My personal's helper

Where's my Password

Password logs

Name

Address

Phone

E-mail

Note

My password

Account :_____

Website/App : _____

User name : _____

E-Mail : _____

Password : _____

Remark : _____

Note :

Note :

Account :_____

Website/App : _____

User name : _____

E-Mail : _____

Password : _____

Remark : _____

Account :_____

Website/App : _____

User name : _____

E-Mail : _____

Password : _____

Remark : _____

Note :

Note :

Account :_____

Website/App : _____

User name : _____

E-Mail : _____

Password : _____

Remark : _____

Account :_____

Website/App : _____

User name : _____

E-Mail : _____

Password : _____

Remark : _____

Note :

Note :

Account :_____

Website/App : _____

User name : _____

E-Mail : _____

Password : _____

Remark : _____

Account :_____

Website/App : _____

User name : _____

E-Mail : _____

Password : _____

Remark : _____

Note :

Note :

Account :_____

Website/App : _____

User name : _____

E-Mail : _____

Password : _____

Remark : _____

Account :_____

Website/App : _____

User name : _____

E-Mail : _____

Password : _____

Remark : _____

Note :

Note :

Account :_____

Website/App : _____

User name : _____

E-Mail : _____

Password : _____

Remark : _____

Account :_____

Website/App : _____

User name : _____

E-Mail : _____

Password : _____

Remark : _____

Note :

Note :

Account :_____

Website/App : _____

User name : _____

E-Mail : _____

Password : _____

Remark : _____

Account :_____

Website/App : _____

User name : _____

E-Mail : _____

Password : _____

Remark : _____

Note :

Note :

Account :_____

Website/App : _____

User name : _____

E-Mail : _____

Password : _____

Remark : _____

Account :_____

Website/App : _____

User name : _____

E-Mail : _____

Password : _____

Remark : _____

Note :

Note :

Account :_____

Website/App : _____

User name : _____

E-Mail : _____

Password : _____

Remark : _____

Account :_____

Website/App : _____

User name : _____

E-Mail : _____

Password : _____

Remark : _____

Note :

Note :

Account :_____

Website/App : _____

User name : _____

E-Mail : _____

Password : _____

Remark : _____

Account :_____

Website/App : _____

User name : _____

E-Mail : _____

Password : _____

Remark : _____

Note :

Note :

Account :_____

Website/App : _____

User name : _____

E-Mail : _____

Password : _____

Remark : _____

Account :_____

Website/App : _____

User name : _____

E-Mail : _____

Password : _____

Remark : _____

Note :

Note :

Account :_____

Website/App : _____

User name : _____

E-Mail : _____

Password : _____

Remark : _____

Account :_____

Website/App : _____

User name : _____

E-Mail : _____

Password : _____

Remark : _____

Note :

Note :

Account :_____

Website/App : _____

User name : _____

E-Mail : _____

Password : _____

Remark : _____

Account :_____

Website/App : _____

User name : _____

E-Mail : _____

Password : _____

Remark : _____

Note :

Note :

Account :_____

Website/App : _____

User name : _____

E-Mail : _____

Password : _____

Remark : _____

Account :_____

Website/App : _____

User name : _____

E-Mail : _____

Password : _____

Remark : _____

Note :

Note :

Account :_____

Website/App : _____

User name : _____

E-Mail : _____

Password : _____

Remark : _____

Account :_____

Website/App : _____

User name : _____

E-Mail : _____

Password : _____

Remark : _____

Note :

Note :

Account :_____

Website/App : _____

User name : _____

E-Mail : _____

Password : _____

Remark : _____

Account :_____

Website/App : _____

User name : _____

E-Mail : _____

Password : _____

Remark : _____

Note :

Note :

Account :_____

Website/App : _____

User name : _____

E-Mail : _____

Password : _____

Remark : _____

Account :_____

Website/App : _____

User name : _____

E-Mail : _____

Password : _____

Remark : _____

Note :

Note :

Account :_____

Website/App : _____

User name : _____

E-Mail : _____

Password : _____

Remark : _____

Account :_____

Website/App : _____

User name : _____

E-Mail : _____

Password : _____

Remark : _____

Note :

Note :

Account :_____

Website/App : _____

User name : _____

E-Mail : _____

Password : _____

Remark : _____

Account :_____

Website/App : _____

User name : _____

E-Mail : _____

Password : _____

Remark : _____

Note :

Note :

Account :_____

Website/App : _____

User name : _____

E-Mail : _____

Password : _____

Remark : _____

Account :_____

Website/App : _____

User name : _____

E-Mail : _____

Password : _____

Remark : _____

Note :

Note :

Account :_____

Website/App : _____

User name : _____

E-Mail : _____

Password : _____

Remark : _____

Account :_____

Website/App : _____

User name : _____

E-Mail : _____

Password : _____

Remark : _____

Note :

Note :

Account :_____

Website/App : _____

User name : _____

E-Mail : _____

Password : _____

Remark : _____

Account :_____

Website/App : _____

User name : _____

E-Mail : _____

Password : _____

Remark : _____

Note :

Note :

Account :_____

Website/App : _____

User name : _____

E-Mail : _____

Password : _____

Remark : _____

Account :_____

Website/App : _____

User name : _____

E-Mail : _____

Password : _____

Remark : _____

Note :

Note :

Account :_____

Website/App : _____

User name : _____

E-Mail : _____

Password : _____

Remark : _____

Account :_____

Website/App : _____

User name : _____

E-Mail : _____

Password : _____

Remark : _____

Note :

Note :

Account :_____

Website/App : _____

User name : _____

E-Mail : _____

Password : _____

Remark : _____

Account :_____

Website/App : _____

User name : _____

E-Mail : _____

Password : _____

Remark : _____

Note :

Note :

Account :_____

Website/App : _____

User name : _____

E-Mail : _____

Password : _____

Remark : _____

Account :_____

Website/App : _____

User name : _____

E-Mail : _____

Password : _____

Remark : _____

Note :

Note :

Account :_____

Website/App : _____

User name : _____

E-Mail : _____

Password : _____

Remark : _____

Account :_____

Website/App : _____

User name : _____

E-Mail : _____

Password : _____

Remark : _____

Note :

Note :

Account :_____

Website/App : _____

User name : _____

E-Mail : _____

Password : _____

Remark : _____

Account :_____

Website/App : _____

User name : _____

E-Mail : _____

Password : _____

Remark : _____

Note :

Note :

Account :_____

Website/App : _____

User name : _____

E-Mail : _____

Password : _____

Remark : _____

Wifi password

Place : _____

Wifi name : _____

User name : _____

Password : _____

Note :

Place : _____

Wifi name : _____

User name : _____

Password : _____

Note :

Place : _____

Wifi name : _____

User name : _____

Password : _____

Note :

Place : _____

Wifi name : _____

User name : _____

Password : _____

Note :

Place : _____

Wifi name : _____

User name : _____

Password : _____

Note :

Place : _____	Note :
Wifi name : _____	
User name : _____	
Password : _____	

Place : _____	Note :
Wifi name : _____	
User name : _____	
Password : _____	

Place : _____	Note :
Wifi name : _____	
User name : _____	
Password : _____	

Place : _____	Note :
Wifi name : _____	
User name : _____	
Password : _____	

Place : _____	Note :
Wifi name : _____	
User name : _____	
Password : _____	

Place : _____

Wifi name : _____

User name : _____

Password : _____

Note :

Place : _____

Wifi name : _____

User name : _____

Password : _____

Note :

Place : _____

Wifi name : _____

User name : _____

Password : _____

Note :

Place : _____

Wifi name : _____

User name : _____

Password : _____

Note :

Place : _____

Wifi name : _____

User name : _____

Password : _____

Note :

Place : _____

Wifi name : _____

User name : _____

Password : _____

Note :

Place : _____

Wifi name : _____

User name : _____

Password : _____

Note :

Place : _____

Wifi name : _____

User name : _____

Password : _____

Note :

Place : _____

Wifi name : _____

User name : _____

Password : _____

Note :

Place : _____

Wifi name : _____

User name : _____

Password : _____

Note :

Place : _____

Wifi name : _____

User name : _____

Password : _____

Note :

Place : _____

Wifi name : _____

User name : _____

Password : _____

Note :

Place : _____

Wifi name : _____

User name : _____

Password : _____

Note :

Place : _____

Wifi name : _____

User name : _____

Password : _____

Note :

Place : _____

Wifi name : _____

User name : _____

Password : _____

Note :

Card password

Account : _____

Card Name : _____

Card no. : _____

Password : _____

Note :

Account : _____

Card Name : _____

Card no. : _____

Password : _____

Note :

Note :

Account : _____

Card Name : _____

Card no. : _____

Password : _____

Note :

Account : _____

Card Name : _____

Card no. : _____

Password : _____

Account : _____

Card Name : _____

Card no. : _____

Password : _____

Note :

Account : _____

Card Name : _____

Card no. : _____

Password : _____

Note :

Account : _____

Card Name : _____

Card no. : _____

Password : _____

Note :

Note :

Account : _____

Card Name : _____

Card no. : _____

Password : _____

Note :

Account : _____

Card Name : _____

Card no. : _____

Password : _____

Account : _____

Card Name : _____

Card no. : _____

Password : _____

Note :

Account : _____

Card Name : _____

Card no. : _____

Password : _____

Note :

Account : _____

Card Name : _____

Card no. : _____

Password : _____

Note :

Note :

Account : _____

Card Name : _____

Card no. : _____

Password : _____

Note :

Account : _____

Card Name : _____

Card no. : _____

Password : _____

Account : _____

Card Name : _____

Card no. : _____

Password : _____

Note :

Account : _____

Card Name : _____

Card no. : _____

Password : _____

Note :

Account : _____

Card Name : _____

Card no. : _____

Password : _____

Note :

Note :

Account : _____

Card Name : _____

Card no. : _____

Password : _____

Note :

Account : _____

Card Name : _____

Card no. : _____

Password : _____

Account : _____

Card Name : _____

Card no. : _____

Password : _____

Note :

Account : _____

Card Name : _____

Card no. : _____

Password : _____

Note :

Account : _____

Card Name : _____

Card no. : _____

Password : _____

Note :

Note :

Account : _____

Card Name : _____

Card no. : _____

Password : _____

Note :

Account : _____

Card Name : _____

Card no. : _____

Password : _____

Account : _____

Card Name : _____

Card no. : _____

Password : _____

Note :

Account : _____

Card Name : _____

Card no. : _____

Password : _____

Note :

Account : _____

Card Name : _____

Card no. : _____

Password : _____

Note :

Note :

Account : _____

Card Name : _____

Card no. : _____

Password : _____

Note :

Account : _____

Card Name : _____

Card no. : _____

Password : _____

Account : _____

Card Name : _____

Card no. : _____

Password : _____

Note :